W9-DDU-134

Grades 2 – 3

WRITING
FRAMEWORKS

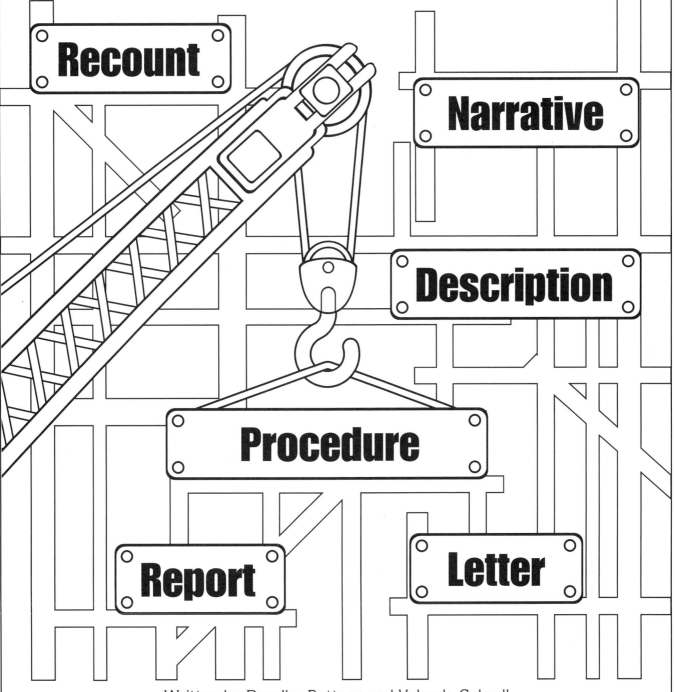

Recount

Narrative

Description

Procedure

Report

Letter

Written by Rosalba Bottega and Yolande Colwell

Published by World Teachers Press®

Order Number 2-5184
ISBN 1-58324-118-3

A B C D E F 03 02 01

395 Main Street
Rowley, MA 01969
www.worldteacherspress.com

Foreword

Writing Frameworks—Grade 2 – 3 is one in a series of three blackline master books designed to familiarize students with writing frameworks through a thematic approach.

Each framework (recount, narrative, letter, description, report and procedure) is based on a different theme and written in a clear step-by-step format. A collection of support activities follows each framework. These activities include:

- writing individual texts in the given framework outline
- comprehension questions
- a variety of word study activities
- cloze

Assessment examples and answers are also provided for your use, and a writing checklist is provided for student self-assessment.

The final section in this book is a learning center to be used independently by students or as directed by you. It consists of writing and creative activities. You may choose to make these activities into individual work cards or simply enlarge the worksheet and allow students to choose an activity. A student response sheet has been provided for each activity.

Other books in this series are:

Writing Frameworks—Grades 4 – 5
Writing Frameworks—Grades 6 – 7

Contents

Teachers Notes

Writing Frameworks—Grade 2 – 3 consists of six original pieces of text each written according to a different framework.

These are:
- recount
- letter
- report
- narrative
- description
- procedure

Each framework is based on a different theme which is made up of six to eight pages.

The following provides an explanation of how to use this book.

The title at the top indicates the theme.

The first page of each theme presents an example of the framework being covered. These are listed on the contents page.

Each framework is written in a clear step-by-step format. Students will need to refer to this page to complete accompanying activities.

The second page consists of comprehension activities based on the framework. Question types include literal, inferential and evaluative.

A cloze activity is the basis for the third page. Students can refer to the first page or fill in appropriate answers for the missing words. This activity promotes thinking and reinforces word study items.

The next two to four pages consist of a variety of word study activities. The main emphasis is listed in brackets on the contents page. Activities include sentence reconstruction, dictionary skills, word building, direct speech, word searches and finding synonyms and antonyms.

The final page of each theme consists of a framework outline for writing individual texts. Students study and discuss the example given on the first page. They then complete their own framework. Teachers may need to give further guidance to certain students depending on his/her ability.

Teachers Notes

Also included is an assessment sheet, writing checklist, learning center and learning center response sheet.

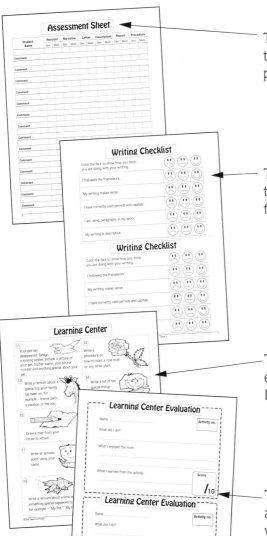

The assessment sheet example on page 6 allows you to record the themes completed by each student and evaluate individual progress.

The writing checklist on page 7 can be distributed to students for them to make their own self-assessment after completing each framework outline on the final page of each theme.

The ideas for the learning center on pages 48 and 49 can be enlarged on a photocopier and made into individual activity cards. It can be used by students independently or as directed by you.

The learning center evaluation sheet on page 50 allows both you and the student to keep track of activities completed and gauge what the student achieved from the activity.

Answers are provided on pages 51 and 52.

Writing Frameworks—Grade 2 – 3 can be used in the following ways:

1. Whole class—with you and students reading the text together and follow-up activities being carefully explained before students attempt on their own.

   Each theme can be gradually completed over a number of lessons or taken home to complete as part of a program.

2. Independently—students who are capable readers can read the text and complete the activities on their own or with minimal guidance.

3. Small group—while capable students are working independently, you can select a small group of less able students who need one-to-one guidance.

Assessment Sheet

Student Name	Recount		Narrative		Letter		Description		Report		Procedure	
	Dev.	Mast.	Dev.	Mast.	Dev.	Mast.	Dev.	Mast.	Dev.	Mast.	Dev.	Mast.
Comment												
Comment												
Comment												
Comment												
Comment												
Comment												
Comment												
Comment												
Comment												
Comment												
Comment												
Comment												

Dev. = Developing   Mast. = Mastered

Writing Checklist

Color the face to show how you think you are doing with your writing.

I followed the framework.	☹	😐	🙂
My writing makes sense.	☹	😐	🙂
I have correctly used periods and capitals.	☹	😐	🙂
I am using paragraphs in my work.	☹	😐	🙂
My writing is descriptive.	☹	😐	🙂

Writing Checklist

Color the face to show how you think you are doing with your writing.

I followed the framework.	☹	😐	🙂
My writing makes sense.	☹	😐	🙂
I have correctly used periods and capitals.	☹	😐	🙂
I am using paragraphs in my work.	☹	😐	🙂
My writing is descriptive.	☹	😐	🙂

Our Day at the Fun Park

Opening Statement (When, who, where?)

Yesterday, Mom took my brother and me to the Fun Park. We caught the train. There were many different things to see when we got there. What would we do first?

Event 1 (Events in time order)

The first things we saw were the clowns. They made us laugh. They did lots of tricks like juggling balls, squirting water at each other, honking their noses and telling jokes. The best part was when the clowns fell off their bikes.

Event 2

Next we went for a ride on the bumper cars. They were great fun. My brother and I were allowed to ride on one car each. We spent the whole time chasing each other around the ring. It was fun listening to people laughing and screaming.

Event 3

After lunch, we bought tickets to the trapeze show. It was amazing. Men, women and children were swinging in the air and balancing on beams. The beams were different heights. My favorite part was when the trapeze artists hung from large springs in the air.

Conclusion (Ending statement)

We had a very exciting day at the Fun Park. By the time we got home, my brother and I were very tired. We were ready to go to bed and dream about our wonderful day.

Our Day at the Fun Park

Use the story to answer the questions.

1. Who went to the Fun Park? _____

2. What was the first thing they saw? _____

3. Why do you think the children wanted one bumper car each?

_____

_____

4. When were the people laughing and screaming?

_____

5. How do you think you would feel if you were swinging through the air?

_____

_____

6. What did the boy enjoy the most at the trapeze show?

_____

7. How do you think the family got home? _____

_____

8. List four things you would like to do if you went to a Fun Park.

_____

_____

_____

_____

9. Draw your favorite part of a Fun Park.

Our Day at the Fun Park

Yesterday, Mom took my brother and me to the Fun Park. We caught the

_____(1). There were many different things to see when

we got _____(2). What would we do _____(3)?

The first things we saw were the clowns. They made us _____(4).

They did lots of tricks like juggling _____(5), squirting

water at each other, honking _____(6) noses and telling jokes. The

_____(7) part was when the clowns fell off their bikes.

Next we went for a ride on the bumper cars. They were _____(8)

fun. My brother and I were allowed to get one car each. We spent the whole time

_____(9) each other around the ring.

It was fun listening to people laughing and _____(10).

After lunch, we bought tickets to the trapeze show. It was

_____(11). Men, women and children were

_____(12) in the air and balancing on beams. The beams were

different _____(13). My favorite part was when the trapeze

artists _____(14) from large springs in the air.

We had a very exciting day at the Fun Park. By the time we got home, my

_____(15) and I were very tired. We were ready to go to bed and

_____(16) about our wonderful day.

Writing Frameworks – Book 1 World Teachers Press®

Our Day at the Fun Park

Choose words from the story to help you find the answers to the following activities.

1. Antonyms are words that are opposite in meaning. Find the antonyms for these words.

   (a) tomorrow _____

   (b) same _____

   (c) sister _____

   (d) boring _____

   (e) last _____

2. Complete the table below to build new words.

Word	Add "s"	Add "ed"	Add "ing"
squirt	squirts	squirted	squirting
joke			
scream			
part			
laugh			
juggle			

3. Add the correct letters from the list to complete these words.

   (a) f i r _____ _____   **e n**

   (b) t r _____ _____ n   **s t**

   (c) l i s t _____ _____   **a r**

   (d) l _____ _____ g e   **a i**

   (e) p _____ _____ t   **a r**

4. Synonyms are words that are similar in meaning. Match the synonyms.

   (a) laugh •   • riddles

   (b) ladies •   • giggle

   (c) jokes •   • best

   (d) favorite •   • sleepy

   (e) tired •   • women

Our Day at the Fun Park

My Clown

by: _____

Name: _____

Lives: _____

Looks like: _____

My clown likes to: _____

_____

My clown's favorite trick is: _____

_____

Interesting habits: _____

_____

Elle the Elephant

by: _____

Lives: _____

Looks like: _____

Elle can: _____

_____

Elle likes to eat: _____

Elle is special because: _____

World Teachers Press®

Writing a Recount

Write a recount about a visit to a Fun Park or a zoo. Tell how you got there and what happened. Follow the layout below.

Title _____

Opening Statement (When, who, what, where and why?)

_____

_____

_____

Event 1

_____

_____

_____

Event 2

_____

_____

_____

Event 3

_____

_____

_____

Conclusion (Ending Statement)

_____

_____

_____

The Three Little Pigs

Setting (When, who, where)

Once upon a time, there were three little pigs who wanted to live in their own homes. Together they went looking at houses.

Beginning Event (What starts the story?)

The first little pig saw a house of straw. He thought that it would be very easy and quick to build. So he did.

The second little pig saw a house of sticks and he thought, "That's for me!" It, too, was easy to build. In no time at all, the two little pigs had built their homes. They were then free to play, sing and dance together.

The last little pig built a house of bricks. It took a long time to build, but he knew that it was very strong. It would keep him safe.

Problem (What makes the story exciting?)

The first little pig saw a wolf coming towards him, so he ran into his house. The wolf followed him and blew the house down. Luckily, the first little pig made it to the second little pig's house. The wolf followed him again. This time he blew a bit harder and the stick house blew down too.

The pigs escaped just in time. Now they all hid inside the brick house. But again the wolf followed them. He tried to blow the brick house down but he couldn't.

Resolution (How is the problem solved?)

The wolf decided to go down the chimney. Luckily the pigs were ready for him. They had a pot of boiling water in the fireplace. When the wolf came down he made a big splash and that was the end of him.

Conclusion (How does the story end?)

Soon afterwards, the pigs built two more brick houses. They all lived happily ever after.

   World Teachers Press®

The Three Little Pigs

Use the story to answer the questions.

1. What was the first little pig's house made of?

_____

2. Why do you think the wolf could blow down the stick house?

_____

_____

3. How do you think the second little pig felt when his house was blown down? Why?

_____

_____

4. Why do you think the wolf couldn't blow down the brick house?

_____

_____

5. Do you think the third little pig helped the other two pigs build their brick homes?

_____ Why/Why not? _____

_____

_____

6. Who was your favorite character? Why?

_____

_____

_____

_____

_____

7. Draw the wolf blowing down the straw house.

The Three Little Pigs

Once upon a time, there were three little pigs who wanted to live in their own homes.

Together they went _____ (1) at houses.

The first little pig saw a house of straw. He thought that it would be

very easy and _____ (2) to build. So he did.

The second little pig saw a house of sticks and he thought, "That's for me!" It, too, was

easy to _____ (3). In no time at all, the two little pigs had built

their homes. They were then free to play, sing and dance _____ (4).

The last little pig built a house of bricks. It took a long time to build, but he knew

that it was very _____ (5). It would keep him safe.

The first little pig saw a wolf _____ (6) towards him, so he ran into

his house. The wolf _____ (7) him and blew the house down.

Luckily, the first little pig made it to the second _____ (8) pig's

house. The wolf followed him again. This time he blew a bit harder and the

_____ (9) house blew down too.

The pigs escaped just in time. Now they all _____ (10) inside the

brick house. But again the wolf _____ (11) them. He tried to blow

the brick house down but he _____ (12).

The wolf decided to go down the chimney. Luckily the pigs were ready for him. They had

a pot of _____ (13) water waiting in the fireplace. When the wolf

came down he made a big splash and that was the end of him.

Soon afterwards, the pigs built two more brick houses.

They all lived _____ (14) ever after.

The Three Little Pigs

Cut out the paragraphs below. Glue them onto a sheet of
paper in the correct order.

Once upon a time, there were three little pigs that wanted to live in their own homes.
Together they went looking at houses.

The wolf decided to go down the chimney. Luckily the pigs were ready for him. They had a
pot of boiling water waiting in the fireplace. When the wolf came down he made
a big splash and that was the end of him.

The last little pig built a house of bricks. It took a long time to build, but he knew that
it was very strong. It would keep him safe.

The first little pig saw a house of straw. He thought that it would be very easy and
quick to build. So he did.

The first little pig saw a wolf coming towards him, so he ran into his house. The wolf
followed him and blew the house down. Luckily, the first little pig made it to the second
little pig's house. The wolf followed him again. This time he blew a bit harder and the stick
house blew down too.

The second little pig saw a house of sticks and he thought, "That's for me!" It, too, was
easy to build. In no time at all, the two little pigs had built their homes. They were then
free to play, sing and dance together.

Soon afterwards, the pigs built two more brick houses. They all lived happily ever after.

The pigs escaped just in time. Now they all hid inside the brick house. But again the
wolf followed them. He tried to blow the brick house down but he couldn't.

The Three Little Pigs

1. Write what you think each character is saying in the speech bubbles.

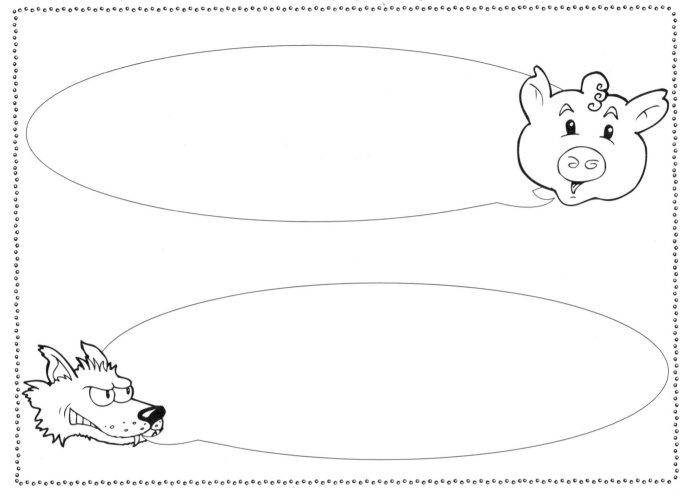

2. Complete the sentences by adding quotation marks.

(a)   Who's that knocking on my door? said the first little pig.

(b)   Help! cried the wolf.

(c)   It will be easy and quick to build a stick house, said the second little pig.

(d)   Little pig, little pig, let me in, growled the wolf.

(e)   The last little pig said, I'm going to build a brick house.

(f)   Let's play! said the first little pig.

(g)   We need to set a trap to catch the wolf, said the third little pig.

(h)   The wolf is coming! shouted the second little pig.

The Three Little Pigs

1. Find these words in the word search below.

pig   blew   together

house   pot   little

wolf   enough   brick

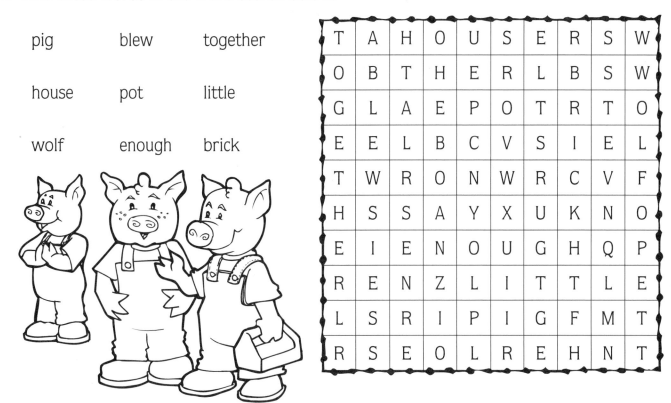

T	A	H	O	U	S	E	R	S	W
O	B	T	H	E	R	L	B	S	W
G	L	A	E	P	O	T	R	T	O
E	E	L	B	C	V	S	I	E	L
T	W	R	O	N	W	R	C	V	F
H	S	S	A	Y	X	U	K	N	O
E	I	E	N	O	U	G	H	Q	P
R	E	N	Z	L	I	T	T	L	E
L	S	R	I	P	I	G	F	M	T
R	S	E	O	L	R	E	H	N	T

2. Use the words from the word search to complete this crossword puzzle.

Make Your Own Puzzle

1. (a) Create your own word search using the grid below.
Choose your favorite fairytale and list 12 words from the story.

_____   _____   _____

_____   _____   _____

_____   _____   _____

_____   _____   _____

(b) Now hide your words in the word search.

(c) Give your word search to a friend to solve. Can they guess the fairytale you chose?

2. Draw a picture of the fairytale that you chose your words from.

Writing a Narrative

Discuss some ideas with a partner. Use this sheet to plan your own narrative.

Title _____

_____

Setting (When, who, where?)

_____

_____

_____

Beginning Event (What starts the story?)

_____

_____

_____

Problem (What makes the story exciting?)

_____

_____

_____

Resolution (How is the problem solved?)

_____

_____

_____

Conclusion (How does the story end?)

_____

_____

_____

Edit your story and write it out on another piece of paper. Illustrate your story.

A Letter from Harry

Address

36 Marian Street
Mt. Lawley, WA 60500

Date

8/24/2000

Dear Andrew,

Introduction (What starts the letter?)

I'm writing to let you know that we have moved to a new house. We are now living in a two-story house with a swimming pool.

Michael and I now have our own bedrooms and we share a study. We also have a game room and a TV room for the whole family to use.

Purpose (Why are you writing?)

I'd like to invite you over to stay for a couple of nights during the school vacation. Mom said that we can go for a swim in the pool and she might take us to the zoo.

Conclusion (How does it end?)

Please ask your Mom and Dad if you can stay. Write back and let me know what they say as soon as possible. I really hope that you can stay. We will have a great time.

Your friend,

Harry Auguston

A Letter from Harry

Use the letter to answer the questions.

1. Who did Harry write the letter to?

_____

2. Where did Harry say his Mom might take them during the vacation?

_____

_____

3. Who do you think Andrew is? Why?

_____

_____

_____

4. Write two reasons why Harry wrote the letter.

_____

_____

_____

5. Do you think Harry's friend would like to stay with him? Why/Why not?

_____

_____

_____

6. Draw a picture of Harry swimming in his pool.

A Letter from Harry

36 Marian Street
Mt. Lawley, WA 60500

8/24/2000

Dear Andrew,

I'm writing to let you know that we have moved to a new house. We are now

_____ (1) in a two-story house with a _____ (2)

pool. We _____ (3) a study. We also _____ (4) a

game room and a TV room for the whole _____ (5) to use.

I'd like to invite you over to stay for a couple of nights during the school vacation. Mom

said that _____ (6) can go for a _____ (7) in the

pool and she might _____ (8) us to the zoo.

Please ask your Mom and Dad if you can stay. Write back and _____ (9)

me know what they say as soon as _____ (10). I really hope that

_____ (11) can stay. We will have a great time.

Your friend,

Harry _____ (12)

Contractions

Contractions are words which are joined together and made shorter by taking out letters and adding an apostrophe. For example, I will = I'll.

1. Join each contraction to its meaning.

(a)	you're •	• it is	
(b)	it's •	• she will	
(c)	who's •	• you are	
(d)	I'm •	• I would	
(e)	we've •	• we will	
(f)	she'll •	• who is	
(g)	I'd •	• we have	
(h)	we'll •	• I am	

2. Finish the sentence for each contraction.

(a) I'd _____ .

(b) We've _____ .

(c) Who's _____ .

(d) That's _____ .

3. Complete the boxes below.

Expanded Form	Contracted Form
	we're
they have	
	there's
	don't
he would	

Invitations

1. Complete the invitation below.

To: _____

You are invited to sleep over at

_____ house.

Date: _____

Address: _____

_____

Time: _____

Please bring: _____

_____

RSVP: _____

2. Design your own invitation to your birthday party below.
Remember to decorate it and include all the necessary information.

Rules for Your Home

1. You have moved to a new house and your family has decided there are going to be rules that must be followed.

With a partner, decide on some rules. List them below.

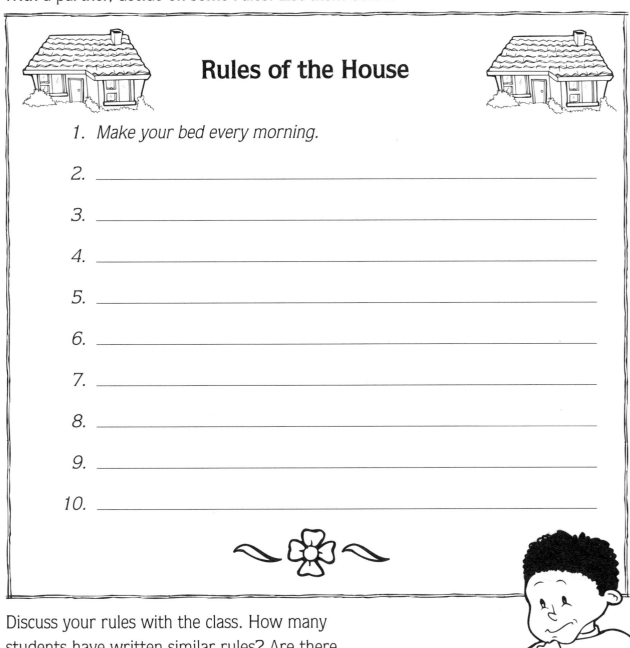

Rules of the House

1. *Make your bed every morning.*

2. _____

3. _____

4. _____

5. _____

6. _____

7. _____

8. _____

9. _____

10. _____

2. Discuss your rules with the class. How many students have written similar rules? Are there any rules that some students disagree with?

3. On another piece of paper, design a rules poster for your bedroom. Decorate it and put it on your bedroom door.

Writing a Letter

Write a letter to a friend. Tell him/her something interesting you have done lately or invite him/her over to stay. Follow the framework below.

Address

_____

Number and Street Name

_____

City, State and ZIP Code   Date

Dear _____

Introduction (What starts the letter?)

_____

_____

_____

Purpose (Why are you writing?)

_____

_____

_____

Conclusion (How does it end?)

_____

_____

_____

From

_____

My Pet Parakeet

Introduction (What is it?)

My pet's name is Peppi. He is a parakeet. Peppi is a special bird who likes to sit on my shoulder and fly around the room.

Description (What it looks like, for example, color, shape, size)

Peppi has a white breast with a blue back and yellow wings. His beak is yellow and his eyes are very dark brown.

Interesting Details (Special features)

Peppi is very clever as he can dance and talk. Peppi likes to say "dance cockatoo, dance cockatoo" (even though he is a parakeet) and he even likes telling people to keep quiet.

Last month we put a mirror and a swing in his cage. He loves looking at himself and sometimes Peppi even swings back and forth.

Conclusion (Ending statement)

Every three months we take Peppi to the vet for a check-up. Sometimes he trims his beak and checks his feet for disease. He's the best pet in the whole world.

My Pet Parakeet

Use the report to answer the questions.

1. What type of pet is Peppi? _____

2. Name two things Peppi likes to do.

_____

_____

3. Why is Peppi clever?

_____

_____

4. When is Peppi taken to the vet? Why?

_____

_____

_____

_____

5. Name three different kinds of animals you could have for a pet.

(a) _____ (b) _____ (c) _____

6. Write the correct color to describe Peppi.

(a) _____ wings

(b) _____ breast

(c) _____ beak

(d) _____ back

7. Draw a pet you own or one you would like to have in the box on this page.

My Pet Parakeet

My pet's name is Peppi. He is a _____ (1). Peppi is a special

_____ (2) who likes to sit on my _____ (3) and

fly around the room.

Peppi has a white _____ (4) with a blue back and yellow

_____ (5). His beak is yellow and his eyes

_____ (6) very dark brown.

Peppi is very clever as he can dance and talk. Peppi likes to

_____ (7) "dance cockatoo, dance cockatoo" (even though he is a

parakeet) and he even likes _____ (8) people to keep

_____ (9).

Last month we put a mirror and a _____ (10) in his cage. He loves

looking at _____ (11) and sometimes Peppi even swings back and forth.

Every three _____ (12) we take Peppi to the vet for a check-up.

Sometimes _____ (13) trims his beak and checks his feet for

_____ (14).

He's the best pet in the whole

_____ (15).

Using "a" or "an"

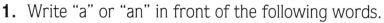

If a word starts with a vowel (a, e, i, o, u), we use "an" before it.
For example, an egg, an orange, an ape.

If a word starts with a consonant, we use "a" before it.
For example, a parakeet, a swing, a mirror.

1. Write "a" or "an" in front of the following words.

(a) _____ elephant

(b) _____ vet

(c) _____ pet

(d) _____ cat

(e) _____ orangutan

(f) _____ zebra

(g) _____ monkey

(h) _____ ant

(i) _____ dog

(j) _____ umbrella

(k) _____ owl

(l) _____ cage

2. Write "a" or "an" in the sentences below.

(a) "This will be _____ easy spelling test," said my teacher.

(b) It turned into _____ sunny day after the dark clouds went away.

(c) Can you think of _____ joke or _____ riddle?

(d) _____ beetle has six legs, but _____ octopus has eight legs.

(e) _____ insect bit me on my left foot.

3. Write a nonsense paragraph below. Include the words "a" and "an" at least twice each. Illustrate your paragraph.

_____

_____

_____

_____

Pattern Poems

Pattern poems follow a rhythmic pattern. Read and follow the example about birds.

Birds

Fluffy birds

Cuddly birds

Cute, precious birds

Colorful birds

Squawking birds

Sweet, singing birds.

1. Write a pattern poem about fish.

Fish

_____ fish

_____ fish

_____, _____ fish

_____ fish

_____ fish

_____, _____ fish.

2. (a) Now write a pattern poem of your own choice.

_____

_____

_____

_____

_____

(b) Ilustrate your poem.

Mixed-up Poems

1. Unjumble each line so the words are in
the correct order and the poem makes sense.

Butterfly, Butterfly

Butterfly, butterfly   _____

air. flies the through   _____

butterfly, Butterfly   _____

everywhere flies   _____

plants the through and   _____

through trees. the   _____

Butterfly, butterfly   _____

sneeze. make me you   _____

2. Now use the poem pattern above to write your own poem about a living creature.
Remember to make lines 2 and 4 rhyme and lines 6 and 8 rhyme. Publish and illustrate
your poem in poster form.

_____

_____

_____

_____

_____

_____

_____

Writing a Description

Write a description about your pet or one that you would like to own. Plan your description using the framework below.

Title _____

_____

Introduction (What is it?)

_____

_____

_____

_____

Description (What does it look like? For example, size, color, body covering)

_____

_____

_____

_____

Interesting Details (Special features)

_____

_____

_____

_____

Conclusion (Ending statement)

_____

_____

_____

Dinosaurs

Classification (What is it?)

The word dinosaur means "terrible lizard." However, dinosaurs were not lizards although they did belong to the reptile family. These animals lived millions of years ago in a world much different from what it is today. All of the dinosaurs are now dead. That means they are extinct.

Description (What does it look like? Color, size, shape)

There were many types of dinosaurs. Some were big and some were small. Some had long necks and others had short necks. Many of the dinosaurs used their legs and tail to defend themselves against their enemies. Some dinosaurs were brown and others were colored green, gray, or black.

Location (Where can it be found?)

Dinosaur skeletons have been found on many continents including Australia, Europe, North America and Asia. They lived in a variety of places, such as in valleys, along rivers, near volcanoes and in swamps.

Dynamics (What can it do?)

Most dinosaurs walked on land, but there were some that could fly or swim. The dinosaurs roamed the land looking for food and water. They tried to keep away from their enemies to avoid fights. Some of the dinosaurs were meat eaters (carnivores) while others were plant eaters (herbivores). Some dinosaurs ate both meat and plants (omnivores).

Summarizing Comment

Dinosaurs were amazing creatures. The king of the dinosaurs was *Tyrannosaurus rex*. He was a mean, large, sharp-toothed dinosaur who fought with other dinosaurs.

Dinosaurs

Use the dinosaur report to answer the questions.

1. What does the word dinosaur mean?

_____

2. When did dinosaurs become extinct?

_____

_____

3. In what kinds of places did dinosaurs live? _____

_____

_____

4. Why did dinosaurs keep away from their enemies?

_____

_____

5. How do we know dinosaurs lived? _____

_____

6. Who was the king of the dinosaurs? Why?

_____

_____

_____

_____

_____

7. Draw and label your favorite dinosaur below.

Dinosaurs

The word dinosaur means "terrible lizard." However, dinosaurs were not

_____(1) although they did belong to the reptile family.

These _____(2) lived millions of years ago in a world much

_____(3) from what it is today. All of the dinosaurs are now

_____(4). That means they _____(5) extinct.

There were many types of dinosaurs. Some were _____(6) and

some were small. Some had long necks and others had _____(7)

necks. Many of the dinosaurs used their legs and tails to defend themselves

against their _____(8). Some dinosaurs were brown and others

were colored green, gray, or _____(9).

Dinosaur skeletons have been found on many continents including Australia, Europe, North

America and Asia. They _____(10) in valleys, near volcanoes, along

rivers and in swamps.

Most dinosaurs walked on land, but there were some that could fly

or _____(11). The dinosaurs roamed the land

looking for _____(12) and water. They tried to keep away from their

enemies to avoid fights. Some of the dinosaurs were meat eaters (carnivores) while others

were _____(13) eaters (herbivores). Some dinosaurs ate both meat

and plants (omnivores).

Dinosaurs were amazing _____(14). The king of the dinosaurs was

Tyrannosaurus rex. He was a mean, large, sharp-toothed dinosaur who fought with

other _____(15).

Writing Frameworks – Book 1 World Teachers Press®

Dinosaurs

1. Draw a line to match the beginning of each sentence to its ending.

(a)	Dinosaurs	•	• meat eaters.
(b)	Some dinosaurs were	•	• lived many years ago.
(c)	*T-rex* was	•	• found on many continents.
(d)	The word "dinosaur"	•	• very large.
(e)	The world of the dinosaurs was •		• fly through the air.
(f)	Some dinosaurs could	•	• means "terrible lizard."
(g)	Dinosaur skeletons have been	•	• very different from ours.

2. Now rewrite each sentence in full below.

(a) _____

(b) _____

(c) _____

(d) _____

(e) _____

(f) _____

(g) _____

3. Unjumble these sentences.

(a) were There types dinosaurs. many of

_____

(b) ate Some dinosaurs plants. meat and both

_____

(c) their They enemies. to tried avoid

_____

Dinosaurs

1. Use a dictionary to find the meaning of these words.

    (a) fossil _____

    (b) reptile _____

    (c) large _____

    (d) lizard _____

    (e) extinct _____

2. Write the following words in alphabetical order.

    (a) dinosaur   ago   many   eat

    _____

    (b) lived   terrible   before   fly

    _____

    (c) lizards   long   plants   millions

    _____

3. Draw pictures of these words in alphabetical order in the boxes below.

    tree   dinosaur   swamp   volcano

Writing a Report

Find out some information about your favorite dinosaur or another animal. Write a report about it following the framework below.

My report about _____

Classification (What is it?)

_____

_____

_____

Description (What does it look like? Color, size, shape)

_____

_____

_____

Location (Where can it be found?)

_____

_____

_____

Dynamics (What can it do?)

_____

_____

_____

Summarizing Comment (What is interesting about this animal?)

_____

_____

_____

Making Bubbles

Topic: Bubbles

Goal: To make bubbles

Requirements: (What is needed)

Ingredients: 1 tablespoon glycerine

1 cup extra strength detergent

$\frac{1}{2}$ cup water

2 teaspoons food coloring

Utensils: bubble-blowing wand

measuring cup

teaspoon

tablespoon

bucket

wooden spoon

Method: (How to do it)

1.   Mix the glycerine and the detergent together.

2.   Add the rest of the ingredients.

3.   Stir thoroughly.

4.   Dip your bubble blowing wand into the mixture and blow.

5.   Repeat with the remaining mixture.

6.   Blow different sized bubbles. (Try blowing softly, quickly, slowly, etc.)

Evaluation: (Did it work?)

Could you blow bubbles that were different sizes?

Making Bubbles

Use the procedure to answer the questions.

1. Write a beginning or ending for each sentence about making bubbles.
   Write the numbers 1–6 in the boxes to show the correct order.

   ☐ (a) Dip your bubble blowing wand into _____

   _____ .

   ☐ (b) _____ thoroughly.

   ☐ (c) Mix the glycerine and _____

   _____ .

   ☐ (d) _____ of the ingredients.

   ☐ (e) Blow different _____ .

   ☐ (f) Repeat with the _____ .

2. Write the ingredient next to the amounts.

   (a) 2 teaspoons _____

   (b) $\frac{1}{2}$ cup _____

   (c) 1 tablespoon _____

   (d) 1 cup _____

3. What do you think would happen if you added only $\frac{1}{2}$ cup of detergent?

   _____

   _____

   _____

   _____

Making Bubbles

Topic: Bubbles

Goal: To make _____ (1)

Requirements:

Ingredients: 1 _____ (2) glycerine;

1 cup extra strength detergent; $\frac{1}{2}$ cup water;

2 teaspoons _____ (3) coloring;

_____ (4): bubble-blowing wand;

measuring _____ (5);

teaspoon; tablespoon; bucket;

_____ (6) spoon

Method:

1.   Mix _____ (7) glycerine and the detergent

_____ (8).

2.   Add the rest _____ (9) the ingredients.

3.   Stir thoroughly.

4.   Dip _____ (10) bubble blowing wand into the mixture

_____ (11) blow.

5.   Repeat _____ (12) the remaining mixture.

6.   Blow different _____ (13) bubbles.

   (Try blowing softly, quickly, slowly, etc.)

Evaluation:

Could you blow bubbles that _____ (14) different sizes?

Compound Words

Compound words are made by joining two separate words. e.g., tea + spoon = teaspoon.

1. Match the words to make compound words.
Write the compound words you made.

(a) day •   • mother   _____

(b) some •   • tale   _____

(c) news •   • body   _____

(d) road •   • light   _____

(e) grand •   • paper   _____

(f) fairy •   • side   _____

2. Draw a picture or write the words for these compound words.

(a) 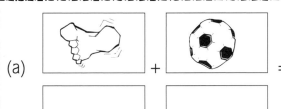 + = _____

(b) ☐ + ☐ = rainbow

(c) 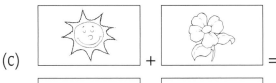 + = _____

(d) ☐ + ☐ = tablespoon

3. Write a sentence for these compound words.

      everyone   **seesaw**   **daylight**

(a) _____

(b) _____

(c) _____

Secret Words

1. (a) Follow the instructions below to work out the secret message.

Take "t" from "out," add "y" to the beginning. _____

Add "c" to the beginning of "an." _____

Join "some" and "times" together. _____

Take "d" from "seed." _____

Add "t" to the front of "he." _____

Take "ing" from "coloring." Add "s." _____

Take "ho" from "hoof." _____

Take "m" from "them." _____

Join "rain" and "bow" together. _____

Add "in" to the beginning of "side." _____

Take "r" and "n" from "ran." _____

Take "n" from "bun." Add "bble." _____

(b) Write the message.

_____ _____ _____ _____

_____ _____ _____ _____

_____ _____ _____ _____.

(c) Make up your own secret message for a friend to solve.

2. Find small words inside each of the words below.

together _____   ingredients _____

wand _____   mixture _____

blowing _____   softly _____

into _____   coloring _____

Writing a Procedure

Make up a procedure for a recipe of your choice. Here are some ideas.

1. How to make playdough.

2. A crazy recipe.

3. Your favorite food.

Topic: _____

Goal: _____

Requirements:

Ingredients:

_____

_____

_____

Utensils:

_____

_____

_____

Method:

_____

_____

_____

_____

Evaluation: _____

Learning Center

These activities can be enlarged on a photocopier and made into individual activity cards.
Standard equipment required is scissors, card, glue, paper, pencils and felt pens.

---

1 Think of your favorite dessert. Write a procedure that tells someone how to make it.

2  Write a letter telling your friend what you did on the weekend. Use the recount framework.

3 Write a report on a farm animal, for example, a pig, a cow, or a chicken. Don't forget to draw your animal.

4  Use the description framework to write about your house or your school.

5 Write a story of your own choice. Remember to follow the narrative framework, for example, "Under the Sea."

6  Read a fairytale. Write a list of questions to ask your friend. Remember to include questions that start with who, what, where, when and why.

7 Design a dinner menu for your favorite restaurant. Remember to include entree, main meal, dessert and drinks.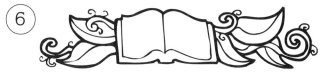

8  Make a postcard and write to a friend. Imagine you are staying somewhere on a vacation. Tell your friend what you have been doing. Write on one side of the postcard and draw a beautiful picture of your destination on the other side.

9 Make a collage out of magazine pictures and then write a description telling what it is about.

10 Design your next birthday invitation. Remember to include who, what, where, time and RSVP.

Learning Center

11 Your pet has disappeared. Design a missing poster. Include a picture of your pet, his/her name, your phone number and anything special about your pet.

12 Write a procedure on how to plant a rose bush or any other plant.

13 Write a recount about a special trip your family has been on, for example – theme park, a vacation, or the zoo.

14 Write a list of ten special things about yourself.

15 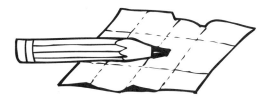 Draw a map from your house to school.

16 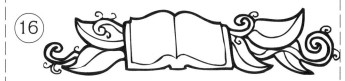 Write out the nursery rhymes you can remember. Illustrate them and make them into a book.

17 Write an acrostic poem using your name.

18  Write a letter to your teacher telling him/her what you are planning for your next birthday party. Remember to format the letter correctly.

19  Write a recount about a time when something special happened to you, for example – "My Pet," "My Vacation."

20  Write a list of your favorite foods. Illustrate.

Learning Center Evaluation

Name _____

Activity no.

What did I do?

_____

What I enjoyed the most:

_____

_____

What I learned from the activity:

Score

_____

/10

_____

Learning Center Evaluation

Name _____

Activity no.

What did I do?

_____

What I enjoyed the most:

_____

_____

What I learned from the activity:

Score

_____

/10

_____

Answers

Our Day in the Fun Park

Page 9

1. Mom and her two children.
2. Clowns.
3. Teacher check
4. When they were on the bumper cars.
5. Teacher check
6. The trapeze artists hanging from large springs in the air.

7–9. Teacher check

Page 10

1. train	2. there	3. first	4. laugh
5. balls	6. their	7. best	8. great
9. chasing	10. screaming	11. amazing	12. swinging
13. heights	14. hung	15. brother	16. dream

Page 11

1. (a) yesterday (b) different (c) brother (d) exciting (e) first

2.

Word	Add "s"	Add "ed"	Add "ing"
squirt	squirts	squirted	squirting
joke	jokes	joked	joking
scream	screams	screamed	screaming
part	parts	parted	parting
laugh	laughs	laughed	laughing
juggle	juggles	juggled	juggling

3. (a) first (b) train (c) listen (d) large (e) part
4. (a) laugh; giggle (b) ladies; women (c) jokes; riddles (d) favorite; best (e) tired; sleepy

The Three Little Pigs

Page 15

1. Straw

2–7. Teacher check

Page 16

1. looking	2. quick	3. build	4. together
5. strong	6. coming	7. followed	8. little
9. stick	10. hid	11. followed	12. couldn't
13. boiling	14. happily		

Page 17

Order from top to bottom: 1, 7, 4, 2, 5, 3, 8, 6

Page 18

1–2. Teacher check

Page 19

1.    2.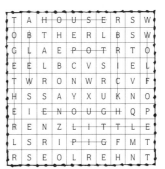

Page 20

1. Teacher check

A Letter from Harry

Page 23

1. Andrew.
2. The zoo.
3. A friend. Because Harry invites him to stay at his house, and he signs the letter "Your friend."

4–6. Teacher check

Page 24

1. living	2. swimming	3. share	4. have
5. family	6. we	7. swim	8. take
9. let	10. possible	11. you	12. Augustson

Page 25

1. (a) you're; you are (b) it's; it is (c) who's; who is
(d) I'm; I am (e) we've; we have (f) she'll; she will
(g) I'd; I would (h) we'll; we will
2. Teacher check

3.

Expanded Form	Contracted Form
we are	we're
they have	they've
there is	there's
do not	don't
he would	he'd

My Pet Parakeet

Page 30

1. A parakeet.
2. Teacher check
3. He can dance and talk.
4. Every three months for a check-up.
5. Teacher check
6. (a) yellow (b) white (c) yellow (d) blue
7. Teacher check

Answers

Page 31

1. parakeet 2. bird 3. shoulder 4. breast
5. wings 6. are 7. say 8. telling
9. quiet 10. swing 11. himself 12. months
13. he 14. disease 15. world

Page 32

1. (a) an (b) a (c) a (d) a (e) an (f) a (g) a (h) an (i) a (j) an (k) an (l) a
2. (a) an (b) a (c) a, a (d) A, an (e) An
3. Teacher check

Page 33

1–2. Teacher check

Page 34

1. Butterfly, butterfly
   flies through the air.
   Butterfly, butterfly
   flies everywhere
   through the plants and
   through the trees.
   Butterfly, butterfly
   you make me sneeze.
2. Teacher check

Dinosaurs

Page 37

1. Terrible lizard.
2. Millions of years ago.
3. In valleys, along rivers, near volcanoes and in swamps.
4. To avoid fights.
5. Their remains have been found.
6. *Tyrannosaurus rex* because he was a mean, large, sharp-toothed dinosaur who fought with others.
7. Teacher check

Page 38

1. lizards 2. animals 3. different 4. dead
5. are 6. big 7. short 8. enemies
9. black 10. lived 11. swim 12. food
13. plant 14. creatures 15. dinosaurs

Page 39

1. (a) Dinosaurs lived many years ago.
   (b) Some dinosaurs were meat eaters.
   (c) *T-rex* was very large.
   (d) The word "dinosaur" means "terrible lizard."
   (e) The world of the dinosaurs was very different from ours.
   (f) Some dinosaurs could fly through the air.
   (g) Dinosaur skeletons have been found on many continents.

2. Teacher check
3. (a) There were many types of dinosaurs.
   (b) Some dinosaurs ate both meat and plants.
   (c) They tried to avoid their enemies.

Page 40

1. Teacher check
2. (a) ago, dinosaur, eat, many
   (b) before, fly, lived, terrible
   (c) lizards, long, millions, plants
3. Teacher check

Making Bubbles

Page 43

1. 4, 3, 1, 2, 6, 5
2. (a) food coloring (b) water (c) glycerine
   (d) extra strength detergent
3. Teacher check

Page 44

1. bubbles 2. tablespoon 3. food 4. Utensils
5. cup 6. wooden 7. the 8. together
9. of 10. your 11. and 12. with
13. sized 14. were

Page 45

1. (a) daylight (b) somebody (c) newspaper (d) roadside
   (e) grandmother (f) fairytale
2–3. Teacher check

Page 46

1. You can sometimes see the colors of the rainbow inside a bubble.
2. Teacher check

MATHEMATICS TODAY

Sample Page from World Teachers Press' *Mathematics Today, Grades 2-3*

WEATHER WATCH

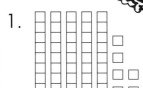

1. 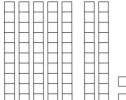 Count the tens: 10   20 _____ _____   50

   Add the ones: 51   52 _____ _____ _____ _____

   56 _____ [_____]   👉 This is the warmest recorded temperature in Alaska (°F).

2. Count the tens: _____ _____ _____ _____

   _____   60 _____

   Add the ones: _____ [_____]   👉 This is the coldest recorded temperature in Hawaii (°F).

3. Count the hundreds: _____

   Add the tens: 110 _____ _____

   Add the ones: _____ _____ _____ [_____]

   This is the hottest recorded temperature in the United States (°F).

Practice Makes Perfect

4. Count by tens:

   (a) 10, 20, _____, _____, _____, _____

   (b) 32, 42, 52, _____, _____, _____, _____

5. Count by ones:

   (a) 25, 26, _____, _____, 29, _____, _____, _____

   (b) _____, 96, _____, 98, _____, _____, _____

MATHEMATICS TODAY

SCIENCE SCENE

Fish	Average Weight in Pounds
Mexican Baracuda	21
Pacific Cod	30
Striped Marlin	494
Blue Shark	437
Golden Trout	11
Walleye	25

1. Which three fish together weigh about 500 pounds?

   _____ _____ _____

2. Name two fish which together weigh about 40 pounds.

   _____ _____

3. How much do:

   (a) 3 Mexican Baracudas weigh? _____

   (b) 2 Blue Sharks weigh? _____

   (c) 4 Walleye weigh? _____

HOME CORNER

Do this project with a family member. Use food advertisements to plan a dinner. You can spend up to $20.00.

4. What did you plan for dinner? List the price for each food item.

   _____

   _____

   _____

   _____

5. How much money did you spend? _____

6. How much money do you have left over? _____

MATHEMATICS TODAY

Sample Page from World Teachers Press' *Mathematics Today, Grades 2-3*

SPORTS REPORT

1. Students at the Osgood School are forming sports teams. Which classes can form complete teams with no left over players? Write a number sentence to show the number of teams.

	doubles tennis (2 players)	basketball teams (5 players)	volleyball teams (10 players)
Miss Kim's class 24 students	yes $24 \div 2 = 12$ 12 teams		
Mr. Donaldson's class 25 students			
Mrs. Baldo's class 20 students			
Ms. Perry's class 26 students			

2. If Mrs. Baldo's class and Mr. Donaldson's class go to gym class together, can all of those students be placed on basketball teams?

   _____

   How many basketball teams can be made? _____

3. Which two classes should be put together so that the students can form volleyball teams? _____

   Explain your choice on the back.

4. Miss Kim's class can be divided into teams of 4 to play Four-Square. Write a number sentence to show how many teams can play Four-Square.

   _____

5. What other class has the exact number to play Four-Square?

   _____

Books Available from World Teachers Press®

MATH

Essential Facts and Tables
  Grades 3-10
Math Puzzles Galore
  Grades 4-8
Practice Math
  Grades 4, 5, 6, 7
Math Speed Tests
  Grades 1-3, 3-6
Problem Solving with Math
  Grades 2-3, 4-5, 6-8
Math Through Language
  Grades 1-2, 2-3, 3-4
Exploring Measurement
  Grades 2-3, 3-4, 5-6
Chance, Statistics & Graphs
  Grades 1-3, 3-5
Step Into Tables
  Elementary
Problem Solving Through Investigation
  Grades 5-8, 7-10
The Early Fraction Book
  Grades 3-4
The Fraction Book
  Grades 5-8
It's About Time
  Grades 2-3, 4-5
Do It Write Math
  Grades 2-3
Mental Math Workouts
  Grades 4-6, 5-7, 6-8, 7-9
Math Grid Games
  Grades 4-8
High Interest Mathematics
  Grades 5-8
Math Homework Assignments
  Gr. 2, 3, 4, 5, 6, 7
Visual Discrimination
Active Math
Math Enrichment
Time Tables Challenges
30 Math Games
  PreK-1
Early Skills Series:
  Addition to Five
  Counting and Recognition to Five
  Cutting Activities
  Early Visual Skills
Spatial Relations
  Grades 1-2, 3-4, 5-6

High Interest Geometry
Money Matters
  Grades 1, 2, 3

LANGUAGE ARTS

My Desktop Dictionary
  Grades 2-5
Spelling Essentials
  Grades 3-10
Reading for Detail
  Grades 4-5, 6-7
Writing Frameworks
  Grades 2-3, 4-5, 6-7
Spelling Success
  Grades 1, 2, 3, 4, 5, 6, 7
My Junior Spelling Journal
  Grades 1-2
My Spelling Journal
  Grades 3-6
Cloze Encounters
  Grades 1-2, 3-4, 5-6
Comprehension Lifters
  1, 2, 3, 4
Grammar Skills
  Grades 2-3, 4-5, 6-8
Vocabulary Development through Dictionary Skills
  Grades 3-4, 5-6, 7-8
Recipes for Readers
  Grades 3-6
Step Up To Comprehension
  Grades 2-3, 4-5, 6-8
Cloze
  Grades 2-3, 4-5, 6-8
Cloze in on Language
  Grades 3-5, 4-6, 5-7, 6-8
Initial Sounds Fold-Ups
Phonic Sound Cards
Early Activity Phonics
Activity Phonics
Early Phonics in Context
Phonics in Context
Build-A-Reader
Communicating
  Grades 5-6
Oral Language
  Grades 2-3, 4-5, 6-8
Listen! Hear!
  Grades 1-2, 3-4, 5-6
Phonic Fold-Ups

Classical Literature
  Grades 2-3, 4-5, 6-8
High Interest Vocabulary
  Grades 5-8
Literacy Lifters
  1, 2, 3 ,4
Look! Listen! Think!
  Grades 2-3, 4-5, 6-7
Teach Editing
  Grades 2-3, 3-4, 5-6
Proofreading and Editing
  Grades 3-4, 4-8, 7-8
High Interest Language
  Grades 5-8
Comprehend It!
  Animal Theme, The Sea Theme, Weird and Mysterious Theme
Comprehension for Young Readers
Language Skill Boosters
  Grades 1, 2, 3, 4, 5, 6, 7
Phonic Charts
Vocabulary Sleuths
  Grades 5-7, 6-9
Early Theme Series:
  Bears, Creepy Crawlies, The Sea
Phonics in Action Series:
  Initial Sounds, Final Consonant Sounds, Initial Blends and Digraphs, Phonic Pictures

OTHERS

Ancient Egypt, Ancient Rome, Ancient Greece
  Grades 4-7
Australian Aboriginal Culture
  Grades 3-4, 5-6, 7-8
Reading Maps
  Grades 2-3, 4-5, 6-8
The Music Book
  Grades 4-8
Mapping Skills
  Grades 2-3, 3-4, 5-6
Introducing The Internet
Internet Theme Series:
  Sea, The Solar System, Endangered Species
Art Media

Visit us at:
www.worldteacherspress.com
for further information and free sample pages.